Seo Marketing Tips

Erik Devash

Seo Marketing Tips

ISBN 978-0-615925950

Table of Contents

What Is Search Engine Optimization, and Why Should I Care?

Picture a beautiful home. For the sake of argument, let's go with white bricks and a cedar shingled roof. And let's say… four bedrooms, three bathrooms, a three car garage, a two acre plot, in-ground pool. The works! Imagine the grounds of this little estate are groomed and manicured to a level of perfection that would have Martha Stewart herself considering stealing a few azalea bushes.

In short, we're talking about most any family's dream home here. And now let's say that this lovely dream home had been constructed a hundred miles north of Bismarck, North Dakota in the middle of absolute nowhere. Guess what? This property? Pool and flower bushes and architectural roof and all? It's pretty much worthless. Any good real estate agent would tell you that, because it lacks the three most important factors when it comes to property. Say it with me: Location, location, and location.

Now picture a top notch website. Picture a site with crisp design, pleasing layout, and excellent navigability between its pages. Imagine this superlative website is rich in wonderfully written content, with writing so captivating that it's worth visiting the site for the text alone, never mind that this website is the homepage of a superlative sporting goods retailer/high end bistro/roller skating rink, a business that people are sure to love of its own volition! Oh, and the graphics on this site? To die for!

Ah but alas, imagine if no one spent any time or effort on optimizing this great website for search engines! Then it may as well be lost in the open plains north of Bismarck. No matter how great your website looks, no matter how well it functions, and no matter the quality of the content on it, if no one can find your site – if search engines like Google and Bing and review sites like Yelp.com aren't driving traffic to your site – then it might as well not exist at all.

Search Engine Optimization, or SEO, in its simplest terms, is the process of making your site more readily "apparent" to search engines; making it easier find. An optimized site can be easily and quickly identified as relevant and respectable by a search engine when the searcher (meaning the actual human person looking for the bistro or the roller skating rink) punches a few simple terms into their browser.

That's what SEO is, in its simplest terms.

A website that is optimized for search will lead to more online traffic, which will lead to more actual business. That's why any business owner or manager should care about Search Engine Optimization. It's just that simple, in theory.

But guess what? As you surely already know (you are reading this book, aren't you?) it ain't actually that simple in practice.

That's why I formed my SEO company (and why I named it Esioh – see? Ess Eee Oh?) in order to help clients make proper use of the essential techniques that make for great SEO. But there are never enough hours in the day to help all the clients I would like to assist with their websites. (In America alone there are well over twenty million small businesses!) Thus I decided to write this book. I can't promise to make you a professional website optimizer over night, but I can promise that by the time you finish this book, you will understand the basic concepts and techniques of good Search Engine Optimization, and you will know how to make your own website that much more optimal. If you choose to undertake your own SEO needs after finishing the book, the more power to you! If you choose to hire someone, confident in the knowledge that they won't be able to talk circles around you and waste your time and money, that's great too!

Like I say, I can't make you a great SEO wizard in just one book. But I can at least convince you of the absolute necessity of Search Engine Optimization for any great website. And I'll bet we can have some fun along the way.

This book is laid out in short, simple chapters that strive to stay narrowly focused for the best clarity of concept. I'm not going to throw around fancy terms when it can be avoided – and there is a glossary – and I won't look down on anyone not skilled in C++ programming or Java or anything like that. Now, let's get started!

Oh, and for the record, I have nothing against North Dakota… the place just happens to have lots of open space, which was optimal for my analogy.

Talking the Talk: A Brief Glossary of SEO Lingo

OK, so as you're the kind of person who reads a book about Search Engine Optimization, I'm going to go imagine that we can relate here using a certain level of elevated discourse; I'll take it for granted that you know such basic terms as "search results" and "copy and paste" and "website." If not, then you might want to take a step back and focus on another topic for now. Or you might want to consider a whole new direction for your life, frankly – maybe something less involved with technology and more in the subsistence farming sector.

Assuming you are already a semi-savvy internet user, let's talk about a few of the terms that you'll be seeing a lot of in the coming pages, just to make sure that we are on the same page!

ADWORDS– Google's proprietary CPC (Cost Per Click) model for text-based advertising in its browser. The amount an advertiser bids determines their ad's relative position within the paid search results, and also factors users' Click Through Rate (CTR) for the ad.

ALGORITHM – The mathematical set of rules a search engine uses to rank listings in response to a search query. Search engines guard their algorithms closely, as they are the unique formulas used to determine relevancy during a search.

BACK LINK – A link to your site from another website. The quantity and quality of backlinks have a huge impact on your search engine ranking. (See also: "Inbound Link.")

BOUNCE RATE – A "bounce" occurs when a visitor only views a single page on your website before clicking away to a new site or closing their browser altogether. Thus, as you can imagine, a high bounce rate is bad, and shows that people are not engaging with your site.

BROWSER – Just to make sure we're clear here, this is the thing you use to "browse" the World Wide Web. Google, Bing, etc... those things. Browsers are AKA "search engines." There, we're clear.

CONTENT MANAGEMENT SYSTEM (CMS) – A web application used to manage and build web sites and edit web content. Popular blogging platform WordPress is a CMS. You will either use a CMS or hire an expert at some point on this SEO journey, no doubt.

CONVERSION RATE – The percentage of visitors to your site who perform a specific desired action after landing on one of your pages. For example, if 100 visitors land on your web page offer of a newsletter subscription, and one person signs up, that's a 1% Conversion Rate. (And no, that's not a good rate.)

INBOUND LINK – A link from one site into another (meaning another site to your site). Links from other sites with high search Authority will improve your SEO. (See also: "Back Link.")

INTERNAL LINK – A link from one page to another within the one website, such as from a homepage to a products or contact page.

KEYWORD – A word that a user might enter in a search. Each web page should be optimized with the goal of drawing in visitors who have searched using specific keywords.

KEYWORD DENSITY – A proportional measurement of keywords embedded in a page's content. High keyword density focuses the page's subject in a way that a search engine's "Spider" understands (see "Spider" below). Search engines may interpret a Keyword Density that's too high as spam, which results in a lower placement in search results, though. There is a sweet spot, and we'll be talking about it later!

LANDING PAGE – Any page that is frequently seen by new, inbound visitors to your website. Look at your website traffic stats and any page getting a constant, heavy flow of visitors is likely to be a Landing Page. All your Landing Pages should be optimized to maximize Conversions.

META DATA (also Meta Information or Meta Tags) – Meta data is information associated with a web page that's placed in the HTML (programming text) but not displayed by the browser for standard users to see. This data that tells search engines what the pages on your website are about. There are a range of Meta Tags, but only a few of which are relevant to search engine Spiders. The most well-known Meta Tags are the Meta Title, Meta Description and Meta Keywords.

NEGATIVE KEYWORD – A term specified by an advertiser telling Google AdWords that they do not want their ad to appear when someone punches that term into Google. For example, if you add the Negative Keyword "-nike" to the keyword "running shoes", the ad will not be displayed if a person searches upon the term "nike running shoes."

QUERY – A Keyword or phrase entered into a search engine or database; AKA a search!

RANKING – Just like in "real life," your rank refers to your ostensible level of relevance and importance online. The better your site is ranked by search engines, the higher up it will appear in their search results. The goal, of course, is for your site to pop up in the first ten results listed by the browser when certain search terms are used.

SEM/SEARCH ENGINE MARKETING – This is essentially advanced, proactive SEO; SEM is the careful seeding of keywords and search terms throughout proprietary websites as well as in advertising and content placed on other sites. It is more involved, specialized process than most small business owners need to engage in, thus we are movin' on!

SEARCH ENGINE OPTIMIZATION – That's what this book is all about, baby. We'll allow the book to work its own magic.

SEARCH TERMS – This one is easy: it's words. Say you were looking for a great place to get some gelato in Macon, GA. What would you punch into Yahoo! or Bing? I'd think you'd type out "gelato Macon GA." And those, then, would be your search terms.

SITEMAP – A special document created by a webmaster providing a map of all the pages on a website to make it easier for a search engine to Index that website.

SPIDER – A program deployed by search engines that browses the internet and collects information about websites as they jump from one link to the next. Google's web Spider is called Googlebot.

TAG – Many web design programs will allow you to "tag" certain words in your content, essentially promoting them to search engines. Too many tags, and they lose gravitas. Too few, and you may fail to catch the proverbial "eye" of that browser. Think of a post about a sale at the gelato shop we talked about above; the author may choose to "tag" the words 'gelato,' 'Macon,' and 'GA' if she were savvy. The inexperienced tagger may on the other hand over-tag, choosing 'great,' 'sale,' 'on,' 'gelato,' etc. thereby reducing the punch of the terms that matter.

UNIQUE VISITOR – A count of individual users who access your web site. If a visitor comes to a web site and clicks on 100 links, it is still only counted as one unique Visit. (Compare with "Visit.")

URL – The web address of a page on your site (example: www.yoursite.com/contact). A URL (Universal Resource Locator) is the address of all documents and resources on the internet. Most search engines look for the keywords in the domain name, folder name and page name. Keywords should be separated by hyphens. Example: http://www.keyword1.com/keyword2-keyword3.html

VISIT – A common website traffic tracking metric measuring an internet user's single session on your website, starting from the instant they first load your site and ending when they leave. During a user session any number of pages may be accessed.

Content is King

How many times have you received an email with a subject line that goes something like "Hello dear friend" or "This is very important for you" or the like? You know these messages; when you bother to open them at all, they say something along the lines of:

Dear Sir/Madam,

It is with great haste and honor that I remind you of the ten millions USD (United State Dollar Bill) that is waiting you in Federalist Paper Bank of Nigeria. You must furnishing to me (Mr. Idi Mugabe, First Secretary of Fed Bank Niger Delta) your information so I can request the request of blah blah blah

I could go on and on (and believe me, I'd love to – those emails are fun to write) but I think the point will be clear enough already. Aside from the fact that the people behind this type of "fishing scam" are attempting to commit fraud and rob you blind, what is the biggest problem with this type of message? That's right: the content is terrible.

A website without great content is like an art museum without great art. Or, even worse, a website chock full of bad content is like a museum filled with junk. Extending this metaphor briefly, even a building designed by the finest architect will only hold the visitor's attention for so long if it is devoid of furniture and decoration; the same can be said of a website.

Even a site constructed with supremely smooth navigation in mind and designed using clarity of layout on each page is sure to see visitors bouncing away from it if there is simply nothing much of interest on those pristine pages. We'll return to that later, the "architecture" and navigation discussion – it's an important topic, but it's both more involved than we should get into quite yet, and, ultimately, less important for basic Search Engine Optimization.

In this chapter, we are not even going to cover keywords, placement of terms, and other such technical SEO practices; rather we're going to focus on the actual honest-to-goodness content that every great website needs.

The more words on your web pages, the more words there are for a search engine to potentially find; that much is obvious. But a little great content is worth much more than a lot of junk. The reasons for this are twofold: first, browsers are well-engineered to find quality, legitimate content. Second, human beings, your desired audience, respond better to quality than to crap (crass... but true).

Finding the perfect amount of content for your site is an equation you will ultimately have to solve yourself, but I can help you think about some of the variables. First, you have to objectively consider the type of business for which your webpage is being designed. If you sell cabinets, then the chances are good that people visiting your site will want to know about the various woods you use, dimensions you offer, shipping times, and so on. They probably won't want to read an essay about woodworking while trying to figure out the price difference between a walnut veneer and a solid pine door. Your content should be clear and concise; extra words here run the risk of being distracting, and distractions lose cabinet sales!

On the other hand, if you run a business specializing in outdoor sporting adventure trips, your potential clientele may love an essay about river rafting written by an experienced guide. They may even love a short story by Jack London (I reference London not only because he was a great writer, but also because most of his work falls into the public domain, a source of content not to be overlooked!). Or perhaps your site is ripe for a forum in which outdoor enthusiast post their questions, anecdotes, etc.

These two examples should be far enough apart to illuminate the overarching point that content must match context, in terms of type and source, so I'll not add others. Besides, you surely know many examples of sites with appropriate quality content that has held your attention; you surely know sites filled with junk that has turned you off right away.

Great content should be considered as value added. Your website needs to accomplish a few goals, such as telling people your hours, location, and menu for a restaurant, your services and rates for a salon, and so on. Beyond those basic necessities, your content – if it's good, of course – can make your website a boon to your business by being a bonus. If a dentist is not only great with her patients in the office, but also has a website featuring a blog so rich in well-written, informative content that even people who have never visited the practice in person are drawn to and impressed the site, do you think that dentist's business is going to grow or to suffer?

Just as figuring out the right amount of content must be left to you, figuring out just the right type of content must also be decided by each business owner (or their trusty web person), but the best way to formulate your plan is to see what the competition is doing that seems to be working. For examples of websites that offer quality value added content, frankly I recommend you start with Esioh.com, because we practice what we preach. You can also try the sale site Woot.com for a superlative example of great content – and don't be intimidated, they hire professional humorists to write for them!

Keywords and Key Terms

Yes, I was tempted to name this chapter "Keywords Are Key" or "Keywords Unlock Success" or some other such awful pun, but I didn't. And the reasons for that are plural. First, all the puns I thought up were indeed awful. Second, when it comes to Search Engine Optimization, keywords are not a matter to be taken lightly. And third, even the word "keyword" is misleading and incomplete from an SEO standpoint. You need to think in terms of both keywords and key terms (AKA "key phrases").

Here's an example for you. If you Google the word "Lead," your top result will be about the metallic element with an atomic number 82 and the symbol Pb on the periodic table. But if you were actually wondering about the qualities that make for good leadership, you would receive no results of any value unless you added the words "how to" in front of "lead." Now, "how to lead?" That will get you search engine results that will get you real world results. (Probably, maybe. No promises – this book isn't about leadership, it's about SEO!)

So you see? It's really not about keywords as much as it is about key terms. And that is especially true for the small business owner, and doubly true for the small business in a large market. For this chapter we're going to pretend there is a shop called Joe's Pizza in downtown Boston, MA. Why Joe's Pizza? Because "Joe" is a prosaic name and pizza is a common offering. Why Boston? Because it's a lovely town, of course! And because there are more than four million residents in the greater metro area, and Boston has a hellofalot of pizza shops. Fortunately for Joe, he has a website and he knows all about great use of keyword and key term placement for streamlined SEO.

First let's start with a few words that Joe hardly needs to worry about: pizza and Boston. If Joe relies on either of these words as standalone keywords, he is wasting his time and wasting space on his website. Now, "Boston pizza," that's a bit closer, as it likely culls San Francisco and most of Europe and Australia and such out of the search, but it barely puts a dent in the crowded field that is the Boston-area pizza market.

No, when ol' Joe is choosing the right keywords and terms for his website, he needs to think more dynamically if he wants to corner a giant slice of the Boston pizza market. See what I just did there? Giant slice? Maybe Joe could use something like that! If he had those words on his website and some of the college kids in this town full of schools decided they wanted to know "where to get a giant slice of pizza in Boston" then maybe Joe would have an edge over the giant's like Pizza Hut and Domino's, see?

If Joe offers any specialties slices or pies, he should make reference to those, as they will set him apart from the competition. Often the best local SEO techniques are based off the same principals as the best way to run a successful small business: if you can't compete in terms of volume or bargain, you can compete in terms of specialty, quality, and hyper-local focus. What if Joe named a pie or a slice after the neighborhood (or even the street, assuming he was on a major road like Boylston or Commonwealth) where Joe's Pizza was located? That way, a search using general terms for pizza and an area would bring up a specific location... Joe's!

Now, moving away from Joe's pizza, giant slices and great prices notwithstanding, let's talk in more generic terms. The keywords and key terms you choose need to apply to your business, your location, and then to the types of things your customer wants that may be ancillary to your specific products/services – think "free Wi-Fi" for a coffee shop, for example. I leave it to you to decide which terms you need to include, and remember which ones not to waste your time with (pizza... Boston).

Of almost equal importance as which words you use are how you use them. I can make this point blissfully short and sweet: be natural. Remember that example from our introduction? The "phishing" scam email? If you try to force keywords into prose where they just don't fit, your content will come across stilted, too. You have to craft content optimized that seems organic, and that's that.

If there is no way to get key terms into your content in a natural, flowing way, consider using bullet points to highlight your "Great Location" or "Discount for Members" or whatever you need to express: at least that approach won't seem sneaky (or downright ham fisted).

One last point for this section: lots of clients ask me about the repetition of keywords. I say that repetition of keywords is just fine whenever it seems natural. If you can have a series of sentences featuring important keywords and also creating a coherent paragraph, go for it! If you're attempt to have a repetition of keywords is going to make you sound like a robot, then lose the keywords and keep the content smooth and clear.

Search Engine Optimizing Your Website's Navigation

Allow me a nautical metaphor:

If keywords are the beacons that the draw distant sailor to your site, it is optimized site navigation that makes the seaman's visit to the island (that, in this metaphor, is your website) a pleasant one.

There, that's all I have to say about site navigation!

Except that actually there's a hellofalot more to talk about here....

Let's start at the beginning, then, and by the time we've worked through this you'll see that my tale of high seas adventure wasn't actually a total shipwreck.

Site navigation is really just what it sounds like: it is the way in which one travels around your site. It is the way in which one clicks on various links to be taken from your homepage to your contact page to your various products or your menu or your blogroll and so on.

The worst possible site, in terms of navigation, will have no internal links at all. A terrible site will have internal links that are broken, hard to find, or inaccurate. A great site, on the other hand, will have permanent links that are functional, simple to understand, and will have any sublinks easy to find and logically arranged. (Don't worry, I'll be breaking all this down for you.)

It's important for you to focus on a well-designed, navigable site for two reasons. The first is that it will make your visitors more likely to stick around and explore your site, and more likely to return thanks to the pleasant "visit" they enjoyed. The second is that search engines tend to explore websites in much the same way as people do: the more easily a site is navigated, the more of the site content the browser will see when on the prowl using those query terms you chose, and the more relevant the site will become based off of the wealth of content found there.

Think of it like this: if you were looking through the window of a shop and saw goods strewn about the floor, shelves in disarray, and the aisles narrow and twisting, you'd be less likely to enter and shop there. On the other hand, if you gazed into a shop with wide, even aisles sporting orderly shelves with neatly arranged goods, you'd be more likely to saunter on in, because it would be both easy and pleasing to navigate your way through the latter shop.

OK, now let's start talking about specifics. The first rule of good site navigation is that the easier, the better. Don't make your visitors have to work to find their way around your site, because they won't do it, they'll just bounce away to some other, easier to navigate site! You need clear, concise links laid out in a logical manner and placed in a logical location.

The two most common approaches to internal link placement are in a bar across the top of the webpage(s), or stacked one on top of another on the left of the page. Why? Simple: we read from left to right, and from top to bottom.

You most important links should come first, meaning all the way to the left or all the way at the top, depending on your link layout. (The exception can be a link at the center of a series of links – make it stand out using font, size, color, or some other design element, though, if you go for this approach.) Generally speaking, you will start with your first link (on the left or top) as a link to your homepage; it is always good to make it easy for a visitor to return to the homepage – which should be a clean, orderly page indeed – from where they will ideally continue the exploration of your site, start shopping for something new, etc.

After that first link, you should essentially lay out your links in descending order of importance. If you are a furniture store, for example, the next most important link might be OUR PRODUCTS, for example, and if you operate a restaurant, perhaps it should go HOMEPAGE and then MENU. You'll want links to a CONTACT US page, a LOCATION page (for brick and mortar businesses only, of course – online businesses need not worry about that one) and so on. I can't tell you which links to include, because I don't know what type of business you run. But I'm sure it's very nice.

What I can tell you is that five to seven seems to be the magic number for these basic, permanent links, the ones that are simple and direct and which usually appear on every page of the site. If you only need four permanent internal links, fine. If you feel you need ten, then you need to hire a web designer and turn over the construction of your site, because you're out of control!

Now, why exactly is it so important that your links are in the order of importance? Like I said earlier, browsers tend to search in much the same way a human would. Thus the first links Google or Bing sees, the more weight they'll assign to them. Every business site is likely going to have a CONTACT US link, so dump it at the end; not every business is a specialty outfit, like that furniture store of yours, so put your best foot forward, and your most important links early.

Ah, but you say a link such as START SHOPPING or OUR PRODUCTS is likely to be too common to attract much more attention than a CONTACT US link, eh? Not so! That's because those types of links can lead not just to another page, but to any number of other pages thanks to drop down menus. In a site with proper "architecture," a link with its own drop down sub-links will feature sub-links that are all programmed with HTML that a search engine can search not only that first link, but all its sub-links. OK, that was a mouthful. Here's another way to look at it:

START SHOPPING could appear to the search engine as (we're going with furniture here) START SHOPPING, SOFA, LOVE SEAT, KITCHEN TABLE, BEDROOM SET and on and on. By placing these sub-links under one of your first links, you are still giving all those terms added weight, i.e. you are putting more key terms out there for a browser to grab onto.

Just a couple more tips, as I think you have probably gotten the hang of this navigation thing by now. Make sure all pages have at least one easy way to navigate away from them other than using a back button. In a decent-sized website, it's unlikely all your pages will have the permanent links of your homepage, but all pages need to have at least some easy way to return to a page that does. Otherwise, rest assured you'll have people closing your site and bouncing away from it, rather than bouncing around within it.

And lastly, don't count on hypertext to do the job of navigation for you. Words like CLICK HERE can only be counted on to work if they are in their own box or floated on top of their own icon, and not merely buried in the body of content.

SEO "Hacks"

The word "hack" has taken on many meanings over the years, and most of them are pejorative. An unskilled workman hacks away with his tools; a screenwriter writer working on a project for a paycheck rather than passion is a Hollywood hack, and so on.

On the other hand, sometimes a "hack" is simply a way to make life simpler and smoother. Anything from a week's worth of pre-selected outfits to advanced computer cord control systems (just going nerdy for a minute, thank you very much) can be thought of as "life hacks." Try Google Imaging that key term, in fact, if you want to see some great stuff!

In our context too there is nothing bad about a hack: in the realm of SEO, a hack is merely a way to get better ranking faster, and to keep your web pages popping up in prime position in browser result pages. The best part about the hacks were discussing in this chapter? There's nothing underhanded or manipulative about them at all: there's no need to be sneaky when you can be clever!

You can't well have a website boasting thousands of Facebook "Likes" and years of ranking history overnight, but you can still take steps that will help your pages rank higher up in search results. The secret is creativity. In fact, you can think of a Search Engine Optimization hack as out-of-the-box SEO.

1. Using YouTube to Get Results

Have you ever noticed that when you search for something on Google, often a video will pop up near the top of the search results? This is often true even when you have not opted to search for videos.

And that video could well be yours. Search engines these days are dynamic creatures, and they seek to bring you not just links to websites likely applicable to your search, but rather bring you those links along with other types of content, such as images and videos. With a little work, your video could wind up atop those search results, meaning effectively you end up on top!

Even newer and smaller businesses can edge their way into the search results of crowded markets by using a well-positioned, well-ranked video. And it's easier to get solid ranking on YouTube than it is on Google! Yes, the actual content of your media clip should be decent, so either spend the time to make something good yourself or the money having something good produced for you. But the real kicker here comes in the video's description and in the comments you can garner: that is the content a browser will be scanning! Also, you can rather unabashedly share a video, and this type of content is more likely to be shared than is a basic website link.

Say you just opened a car wash in Austin, TX. You have a lot of Texas-sized competition there, for sure. And even a spiffy website repeating the terms "Austin car wash" dozens of times likely won't do much to help you rank against older, established car washes. But what if few (or none!) of the competing car washes near your location had taken the time to produce a video? What if your video had a concise description below it that listed your business's name, location, and services? Maybe your brand new Austin, TX car wash would still be way far down in the web search results, per say, but if you could get your video to pop up on that first page of results, and if your video/video description featured all the info a potential customer could need... then you just hacked your way into the market!

2. Get Your Picture(s) Out There on Google... and Bing and More

It is harder to get an image ranking than a video, because there are millions more images online than there are videos. But it is also much easier to create and upload images than videos. You can get photos of your business online via myriad popular platforms. You should find a great picture or you should use your logo and upload it to Twitter, Facebook, and all other social media platforms with which you are comfortable.

And if you have never used Google+, now is the time! It's easy to follow the step-by-step instructions provided when you begin creating a Google+ account, and the content and images on your Google+ account will, not surprisingly, trend higher on Google than will media from other social media platforms. Create your Google+ account, and then try to form as many connections (called getting people in your "circle") as possible.

Another great way to get your images out there is to...

3. Use Yelp.com and Use it Well!

Yelp.com is so damned important for small businesses these days, I went and wrote a whole book about it. As you might gather from that book's title, Frustrated With Yelp?, it can also be a headache navigating the ins and outs of this website-cum-cultural force. But you can't afford to ignore Yelp.com, not if you want your small business to succeed!

As I already wrote that other book all about Yelp, I'll not go on and on about how to use the site in and of itself, but I will say that getting a business well-ranked and frequently reviewed on Yelp is a great way to get it increased rankings on web browsers. Just as Yahoo! and Google like to pull up videos and images along with their web search results, they like to grab at Yelp pages, too. So if you can get lots of reviews and great ratings for your small business on Yelp.com, you can count on better rankings on Google, Bing, et al. And that can mean more real world business, which means more Yelp reviews which so on and so forth, you get it!

SEO Samples: The Good, the Bad, and... Actually That's It

We have come to the moment when it's time to stop talking about what makes for good SEO content or bad search engine optimization techniques. It's time to start showing you the real deal. When I set out to write this book I wasn't attempting to reveal a bunch of search engine optimization secrets; SEO secrets don't really exist. Rather I was determined to create an honest, straightforward guide to search engine optimization. I wanted to identify a number of proper SEO techniques and clarify how to use search engine optimization to the best possible degree while still making sure your website's content was relevant and well-written – after all, relevant and well-written content is itself a part of good SEO!

So now I'll step aside and let these samples to the talking. After the samples, we'll briefly discuss which passages are examples of good search engine optimized content and which are example of content so poorly optimized for browsers that it's actually doing a disservice (remember: a search engine gets turned off by bogus or terrible content just like a person would).

Oh, and for the record, yes, the first paragraph of this chapter? Yeah, that's some damn fine search engine optimized content right there. Points to you if you noticed, points to me if you didn't!

(Also for the record, the names of the businesses and/or products in this chapter are fabricated!)

1.

If you are looking into renting ski equipment and you will be in Aspen, then Dave's Ski Gear is the spot for you. Aspen is respected as one of the best mountains for skiing anywhere in the country. But to get the most out of your skiing when you visit Aspen you need to have the best ski equipment you can. Why buy skis and poles and boots and such when you can rent these items instead? Dave's Ski Gear assures you that everything you rent from Dave's Ski Gear will be in great shape and yet will cost you just a fraction of what it would cost to purchase, even if you ski for days and come back to Aspen year after year. Dave's Ski Gear has the gear for you.

2.

Before the opening of Family Thai, Boston could claim to have many fine restaurants, but it could not claim to have great Thai cuisine. Now that this charming little Thai restaurant on Beacon Street has opened its doors, Boston dining options have grown not only by a single restaurant, but by a category: authentic Thai food. Downtown Boston now offers diners a taste of downtown Bangkok. But more than bringing to Boston Thai food such as most Thai restaurants offer, Family Thai goes a step further, offering not only such staple Thai dishes as Pad Thai and Panang Chicken, but also offering flavors and preparations from rural Thailand. You can get a taste of Thai home cooking in Boston that would have any native of the country wondering if you had flown it right in from their grandmother's stovetop: that is what sets

Family Thai apart from any other Thai restaurant in Boston: the chefs not only prepare classic Thai cuisine, they specialize in authentic Thai food, offering Bostonians a taste of home right at their new home on Beacon Street.

OK, now let's break this down some. The first sample paragraph (1) is indeed the bad SEO writing. But it's not bad SEO content just because the writing itself is poor, though that certainly is a factor. The main problem with the writing is that the author has broken up the key terms on multiple occasions! There is a lot of skiing-related content written about Aspen, so one needs to be specific, never placing words between the name of the town (Aspen) and the business at hand (Dave's). The even bigger failure comes from placing words between "Aspen" and "ski equipment," though: the author has essentially erased any chance that a casual searcher will ever find poor little Dave's, because now their browser, looking dutifully for ski gear in Aspen, will not even realize that this content is not about two separate things, i.e. ski gear in Aspen, as opposed to ski gear *and* Aspen.

Sample two (2) is good SEO writing primarily because it is solid writing in and of itself: this (totally fabricated, of course – don't go looking for Family Thai on Beacon Street in Boston!) writing could be from a restaurant's website just as easily as it could be from a magazine or website devoted to dining. Every instance of keyword/key term use comes in a natural context and in a flowing (and proper) sentence. By discussing the restaurant in a larger context – the cuisine scene of Boston writ large – this content manages to use many specifics related to Family Thai and also managed to use terms that help place the restaurant (Boston; Beacon Street) on the map... and in the search results. Someone using Google or Bing or Yahoo! to look for Thai food in the Boston, MA area in general may well find this content and be led to Family Thai; someone Googling Family Thai looking for this specific business would surely find what they were looking for. And hell, someone who happened to look for the words "Family Thai" would likely soon know that there was a spot in Beantown just right for them!

A Few Final Thoughts

So there you have it! You should now consider yourself well-versed in the dynamic art of Search Engine Optimization*. I would recommend reading through this guidebook several times before you endeavor to create your own optimized website and/or content. If you simply wanted to learn more about the topic for interest or before hiring someone to help you with your site, then you should be all set.

As I said earlier on in this book, there really is no secret to good SEO; there are no tricks, and anyone looking to gain traffic by using trickery (keyword stuffing or automatic redirects and such) must know their site (and likely their actual business) lacks the substance to merit legitimate visitors/customers: they should be busy changing the way they approach life, not trying to change the way people approach their websites.

Good Search Engine Optimization is the equivalent of a well-manicured lawn and garden, a clean, pressed suit, or an orderly, welcoming reception area: it is not a way to trick people into landing on your site, it is a way to invite people in and to convince them to stay thanks to quality design and content, not thanks to shenanigans.

If you want to learn more about SEO, and if you want to get truly comfortable with creating and using great content and web design, my advice to you would be along the same lines as a professor of creative writing would give to his students: great writers are great readers. Now, you don't have to reach for Tolstoy or Faulkner in order to create great text for your website (not that it would hurt, of course); you just need to spend time seriously studying a handful of great sites. I recommend www.Woot.com for an example of consistently great content. For an example of a site with excellent navigation, try good old www.NPR.org, a site that manages to be chock full of content yet always crisp looking and easy to browse.

Look also, of course, for terrible websites. But don't just write them off, really navigate them and see what specifically is not working or is frustrating. Learning what to avoid is every bit as important as learning what to emulate when designing a website that is properly search engine optimized.

The best thing to remember is that without something worth selling (or without content worth reading or images worth viewing and so on), you can't fool most people into buying. Your best bet when it comes to optimizing your website is to make it simple for people to find out who you are, what you offer, and how to get it: use as much text as you need, get those keywords and key terms in there, and place links where logical (on other sites or in ads), but don't overdo it on any front.

Just keep browsing the web and keep taking note of what you like and what's working for you. Then take the same ideas and put them to work for you and your business.